W9-CYH-341

JP. Keep
© 2017

MEDICAL
DISCOVERIES

STEM: SHAPING THE FUTURE

ARTIFICIAL INTELLIGENCE

COMPUTING AND THE INTERNET

GENETIC ENGINEERING

MEDICAL DISCOVERIES

STEM

» SHAPING THE FUTURE

MEDICAL DISCOVERIES

BEATRICE KAVANAUGH

MASON CREST

Mason Crest
450 Parkway Drive, Suite D
Broomall, Pennsylvania 19008
(866) MCP-BOOK (toll free)

©2017 by Mason Crest, an imprint of National Highlights, Inc.
All rights reserved. No part of this publication may be reproduced or transmitted in any form or by any means, electronic or mechanical, including photocopying, recording, taping, or any information storage and retrieval system, without permission from the publisher.
Printed and bound in the United States of America.
CPSIA Compliance Information: Batch #STFM2017.
For further information, contact Mason Crest at 1-866-MCP-Book.

First printing
1 3 5 7 9 8 6 4 2

on file at the Library of Congress
    ISBN: 978-1-4222-3710-6 (series)
    ISBN: 978-1-4222-3714-4 (hc)
    ISBN: 978-1-4222-8076-8 (ebook)

QR CODES AND LINKS TO THIRD-PARTY CONTENT

TABLE OF CONTENTS

KEY ICONS TO LOOK FOR:

 Words to understand: These words with their easy-to-understand definitions will increase the reader's understanding of the text while building vocabulary skills.

 Sidebars: This boxed material within the main text allows readers to build knowledge, gain insights, explore possibilities, and broaden their perspectives by weaving together additional information to provide realistic and holistic perspectives.

 Educational Videos: Readers can view videos by scanning our QR codes, providing them with additional educational content to supplement the text. Examples include news coverage, moments in history, speeches, iconic sports moments and much more!

 Text-dependent questions: These questions send the reader back to the text for more careful attention to the evidence presented there.

 Research projects: Readers are pointed toward areas of further inquiry connected to each chapter. Suggestions are provided for projects that encourage deeper research and analysis.

 Series glossary of key terms: This back-of-the book glossary contains terminology used throughout this series. Words found here increase the reader's ability to read and comprehend higher-level books and articles in this field.

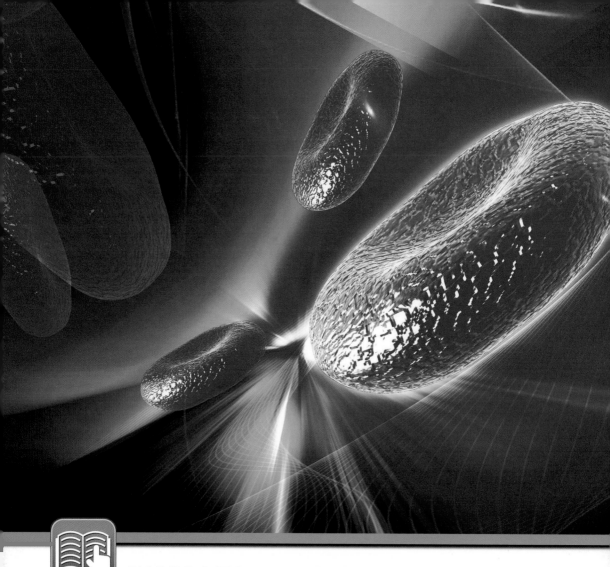

WORDS TO UNDERSTAND

ethical—involving questions of right and wrong behavior

side effect—an often harmful and unwanted effect of a drug or chemical that occurs along with the desired effect

vaccination—the introduction into humans or domestic animals of microorganisms that have previously been treated to make them harmless for the purpose of development of immunity

CHAPTER 1

INTRODUCTION TO HEALTH CARE

WHEN WE ARE ILL OR INJURED, we expect those caring for us to do all they can to make us better. As medical science grows, treatment options and the professionals who can deliver them become more varied, more advanced, and more effective. But can modern medicine present new problems too?

New methods of treating diseases are often complicated and expensive. On top of concerns about the rising costs of health care, medical interventions may have been developed in ways that make people raise *ethical* questions—about whether choices are right or wrong. There are also patients who do not want the treatments they are recommended to take—or they may prefer no treatment at all. How much say should we have in what we allow medical professionals to do?

In this book, we will look at the many ways we treat the sick and consider some of the questions medical interventions raise. The topics are complex—there may not be "right" answers to the issues—but they are important to explore if we are to have an informed say in the future of health care.

Modern medicine is a complex science—it doesn't just involve doctors and nurses. Researchers and lab technicians also play a vital part, developing new drugs and lifesaving procedures.

Medical advances in many fields, such as prosthetics and organ transplants, have enabled people to live much different lives than they would have been able to even 25 years ago.

This book will not tell you what to think. It will give you some scientific background and present different perspectives and ideas to consider. Then you can think about and discuss the issues, forming your own opinions and being able to speak intelligently about them.

PROGRESS IN RESEARCH

Medical researchers are constantly pursuing new ways to treat illnesses, care for patients, and help people to have long and healthy lives. We can now cure diseases that we could not previously, lessen pain, and use tiny pieces of machinery or even body parts from people who have died to replace unhealthy limbs or organs. We can keep seriously ill people alive against all odds, which raises the question—should we prolong life at any cost?

Medical discoveries are the products of hard work and smart decisions, with scientists spending a lot of time and money researching diseases and developing new treatments. Like the rest of the health care field, research is an area with many controversial questions: Some of the research involves the use of material from dead bodies, animals, or fertilized human eggs that have not yet grown into babies. Is it right to use these sources for study?

The treatments developed are tested for a long time on animals and humans, but some object to these processes. How can we decide what is acceptable? Most new treatments and pieces of medical equipment are developed by commercial businesses. These companies need to make money from their work, or they will not be able to fund new research. But many medical companies are often very rich—does this mean they are charging too much? What can we do to make expensive treatments available to people who cannot afford them—to those in developing countries, for example?

THE ROLE OF GOVERNMENT IN HEALTH CARE

Governments play an important role in health care. As well as allocating money to medical services and educating people to live healthy lives, they also have responsibility for other factors in society that affect our health. These can be anything from farming and food-processing methods to traffic control, pollution, and other environmental problems.

Many worry that health problems may be caused by substances like lead and other poisons in fuel, crop pesticides, antibiotics fed to farm animals, genetically modified foods, mobile-phone transmitters, long-distance air travel, living near electricity pylons, and many other factors. We can control some of these ourselves—for example, by living in safer locations or not smoking—but others are beyond our control as individuals, and we need our government to act on our behalf.

CITIZENS AND HEALTH CARE

Why should you worry about health care issues? If you are not ill and your family has no health problems, it may seem unimportant to you. But most of us need medical attention at some point in our lives, and it is in all of our interests to help protect the health of society as a whole. Health care is not just an issue when we are ill. How we live our lives affects our health and that of others. Thus, we can all contribute to global health care.

In many areas of life, we have to balance the needs of different people groups. Medical care presents various problems of this type. Is it better to spend limited funds on prolonging the life of

SIDEBAR

THE LAW, MEDICINE, AND FLIGHTS

Often, it becomes obvious that there is a health risk only when people start to suffer. Medical issues then spill over into legal issues. Some airplane passengers who suffered blood clots believed that their problems were caused by sitting in cramped airplane seats for long periods of time. They sued the airlines for this. Some relatives of passengers who have died are trying to get compensation as well. Is it fair to blame an airline when passengers have opportunities to stand up and move during a flight?

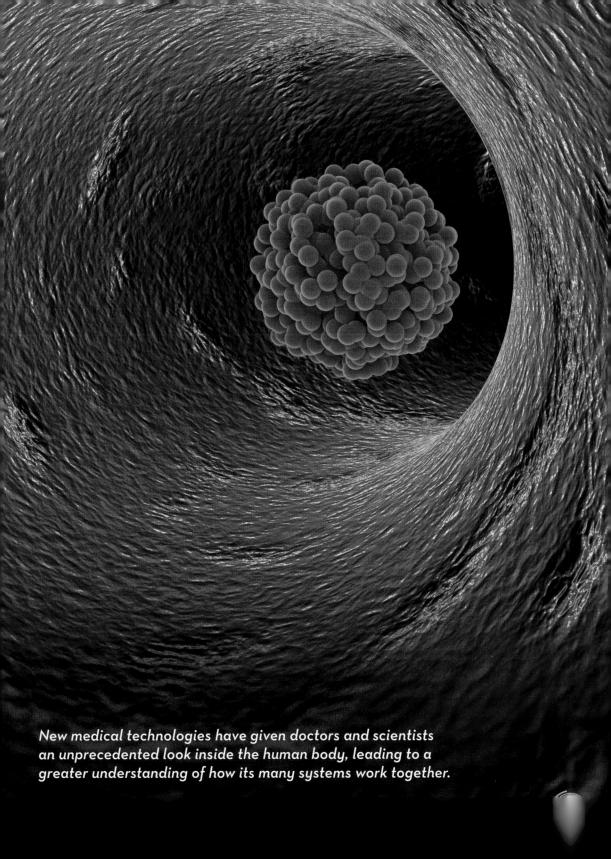

New medical technologies have given doctors and scientists an unprecedented look inside the human body, leading to a greater understanding of how its many systems work together.

one person or on easing suffering for many? Should we insist on people having *vaccinations* to prevent them from getting a disease, thereby protecting the public, or should everyone be free to choose whether or not to be vaccinated? Does someone who has caused their own ill health deserve the same free treatment as another who could not help their condition?

A GLOBAL PERSPECTIVE

Some people live in such appalling conditions that they have no chance for good health in the long run. Is this a local or international responsibility? In the developing world, standards of health and medical care are much lower than in the developed world. Millions of people die because of starvation, polluted water supplies,

A doctor from the United Nations vaccinates a woman and child against tetanus during a mission in the Democratic Republic of the Congo. In many parts of Africa, lack of food and safe drinking water leads to widespread ill health.

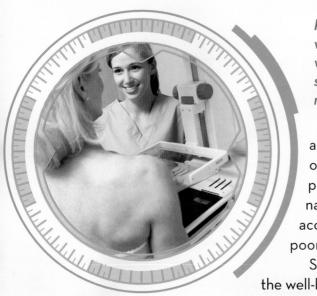

Free screenings have meant fewer women get breast cancer—but many women don't take up the offer of screening. Should such screenings be made compulsory for all women?

and diseases that could be cured or prevented. People suffer health problems as a result of war and natural disasters. Who should be held accountable for health care concerns in poorer countries?

Some of the choices we make affect the well-being and health of people far away. Many in the developing world work in intolerable conditions making goods sold in developed countries, for instance. Sweat shops in the developing world cause health problems for many people. Should we provide health care for people who suffer while making the things we buy or not buy them in the first place? As global citizens and consumers who make choices about what we buy, we can make an impact.

MAKING A DIFFERENCE

Many scientific developments may hold dangers of which we may never know anything about. Some types of medicine or treatment could have consequences we cannot imagine. We have seen a few medical disasters in past years—people contracting AIDS from blood transfusions or new cures with serious *side effects* that bring unintended consequences, for example. We cannot be sure that some of the techniques we are trying now are entirely safe. Does the possibility of danger mean that some procedures or treatments should not be tried? Who should decide?

We all have a right to be involved in decisions about the world's future. But in order to have the power to change things, we need to understand the issues that affect us all. We need to be able to separate fact from opinion in the things we read and hear, and we must disentangle reliable information from media scare stories and public relations hype. If we can do this and shape our own informed views, we will be able to play an important part in the changing world of health care.

TEXT-DEPENDENT QUESTIONS

1. What are three controversial sources of material used in medical research?

2. Name three areas in which a government can influence public health.

EDUCATIONAL VIDEO

WEARABLE DEVICES
FOR MEDICAL CONDITIONS

- Diab...
- Ca... ...ease
- Ol...
- Ep...
- Slee...

CBS THIS MORNING | A HEALTHY NEW YEAR
DR. AGUS ON MEDICAL STORIES TO WATCH FOR IN 2016

Scan here to watch a video on medical innovations.

RESEARCH PROJECT

Using the Internet or your school library, research the topic of vaccines, and answer the following question: "Should vaccinations for known diseases be required of all children?"

Some say the government should mandate vaccinations for all children in order to protect the public and end as many diseases as possible. It is not a matter of personal choice when it could potentially impact many others in serious ways. If polio can be eliminated forever with vaccinations, why would we not do so?

Others contend that it is wrong to force people to get vaccinations because it should be a choice given to each individual or family. There may be some whose religion does not allow for medical interventions or others who are worried about side effects from vaccines. The government does not have the right to require vaccines for all children.

Write a two-page report, using data you have found in your research to support your conclusion, and present it to your class.

📖 WORDS TO UNDERSTAND

abortion—the termination of a pregnancy with the death of the embryo or fetus

conceive—to become pregnant

conception—the process of becoming pregnant involving fertilization or implantation or both

consent—to agree to do or allow something : to give permission for something to happen or be done

embryo—a human or animal in the early stages of development before it is born, hatched, etc.

fetus—a developing human from usually eight weeks after conception to birth

gene—a part of a cell that controls or influences the appearance, growth, etc., of a living thing

gene therapy—a way of treating some disorders and diseases that usually involves replacing mutated copies of genes with healthy genes that have been engineered

induce—to cause (someone or something) to do something

in vitro fertilization—fertilization of an egg in a laboratory dish or test tube; specifically, fertilization by mixing sperm with eggs surgically removed from an ovary followed by implanting one or more of the resulting fertilized eggs in a uterus

miscarriage—a condition in which a pregnancy ends too early—especially between the 12th and 28th week of gestation—and does not result in the birth of a live baby

mutation—a relatively permanent change in genetic material

pro-choice—believing that pregnant women should have the right to choose to have an abortion

pro-life—opposed to abortion, believing that the unborn child is a human being

stem cell—a simple cell in the body that is able to develop into any one of various kinds of cells (such as blood cells, skin cells, etc.)

CHAPTER 2

ISSUES OF NEW LIFE

ONE SUBJECT THAT PEOPLE FEEL very strongly about in health care is babies—how we help people who cannot easily have children, how we cure sick infants, and what we can do about difficult pregnancies.

FERTILITY TREATMENTS

People who cannot have a child of their own naturally will often try interventions—even if they are difficult, unpleasant, or expensive—to help them *conceive*, or become pregnant. Many use fertility drugs—medicines to boost their supply of sperm or eggs or to increase their chances of a new life developing successfully in the womb.

Treatment may also involve taking an egg from the woman or from another woman (an egg donor) and fertilizing it outside the body. This means combining it with sperm, either from the woman's partner or from another man (a sperm donor). A fertilized egg—called an *embryo*—that has the potential to develop into a baby is put back into the woman's womb. If the embryo sticks to the lining of the womb and grows, pregnancy results. This

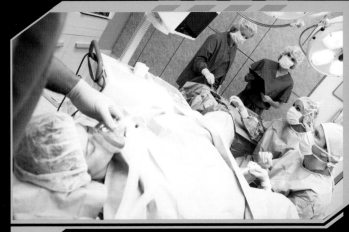

People with fertility problems may be desperate for a baby. But are all the treatments ethical?

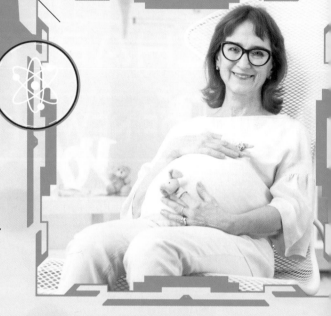

Should older women try to have babies? Should doctors help them to?

process is called *in vitro fertilization*, or IVF.

IVF may be used if either the man or the woman has a fertility problem—if they cannot produce sperm or eggs properly, for example. Or it may be used if one or both partners has a dangerous inherited disease. In this case, sperm or egg donors who do not have the disease can be used. The couple may alternatively use their own eggs and sperm but have the embryos tested, with only healthy ones put back into the womb.

ETHICS IN FERTILITY

Some people feel that fertility drugs should not be used, and IVF should never be carried out because they interfere with the natural processes of conception and birth. But banning these treatments would leave many people who desperately want to have babies unable to fulfill their hopes.

Some believe that fertility treatment is acceptable in many circumstances but object to its use in particular cases: After a woman reaches the menopause, usually around her late 40s, she is no longer able to become pregnant naturally. Men, on the other hand, can become fathers into old age. Using IVF and a donor egg, doctors can enable an older woman to have a baby. This raises serious concerns about the physical fitness of the mother and how she may cope as she and her child grow older.

FERTILIZED EGGS AND EMBRYOS IN IVF

IVF is expensive and does not work every time. To reduce the cost and distress of extra treatment, it is common to fertilize more eggs than necessary when starting an IVF program.

To increase the chances of success, two or three embryos are often put back into the woman's body at once. This means there is a greater chance that IVF will lead to a multiple birth—having more than one baby at a time. For this reason, couples using IVF more commonly have twins or triplets than couples who get pregnant naturally.

Not all the embryos from an IVF program are put into the woman's body. Extras are kept frozen so that they may be used later—if the first treatment does not work or if the couple wants more children. Often, these embryos are never required. Some "leftover" embryos are destroyed while others may be used in medical research.

Difficult questions can arise when a couple does not use all the embryos that have been stored. There have been disputes in recent years when a couple has split up, and one or other has wanted to destroy them. Or the woman has wanted to use an embryo to create another baby, but the man did not want her to. Others question if destroying an embryo is killing a human life.

PREDICTING GENETIC DISORDERS

Some diseases are passed down through families in their *genes*, the chemical "instructions" that determine our individual characteristics. People with a genetic disease used to have a difficult choice to make. Should they avoid having children at all, or should they take their chances and hope

"Spare" IVF embryos are frozen for future use. Who should decide what happens to them if they're not wanted later on by the parents?

SIDEBAR

GENE THERAPY FOR CYSTIC FIBROSIS

Cystic fibrosis (CF) affects about 1 child in every 2,000. The gene that causes it has been identified as the one that contains the instructions to make the natural slimy mucus that protects the insides of the lungs. But the mutated gene makes the mucus much thicker than normal, clogging the lungs and causing coughing, infections, and many other health problems.

There is a genetic test for CF, so a couple can tell before conceiving whether either or both of them has one of the genetic abnormalities that cause CF. If they both have a CF gene, which is recessive, there is a one in four chance their child will have CF. A couple with a CF gene may choose to test the mother's eggs for the gene, test during pregnancy, use donated sperm or eggs without the gene, or not test if they would rather not know.

If parents find that their child has CF, one treatment option is gene therapy, which aims to add the normal mucus-making genes to cells in the lungs with "carriers" such as genetically engineered viruses. However, successful treatment is proving to be difficult: Some lung cells take up the new genes and use them for a time, but eventually, these healthy cells wear out and die. They are replaced by cells with the mutated gene, and the problem comes back.

their children will not inherit the disease? Genetic disorders vary greatly in the ways that they are passed from parent to child and in their effects on health and well-being. But now there are many ways to predict them, detect them if they occur, and treat them.

Sometimes genetic disorders can be predicted by experts called genetic counselors. Genes occur in pairs, and it is possible that one gene of the pair is *mutated*, or altered, while the other is normal. Without undergoing tests, a parent might not be aware that he or she "carries" a mutation that might be passed on to their baby. If an inherited condition has already occurred in the parents' families, the genetic counselor may be able to determine the chances that their baby will have it as well. This may be stated accurately in straightforward terms—for instance, a "three-in-four" risk. If only one parent has the disorder, or it has occurred only in relatives such as brothers or aunts, as opposed to parents, the risk may be less. Sometimes a counselor advises parents to have tests on their blood or other body parts.

TREATMENT OF GENETIC DISORDERS

Some genetic disorders can be detected and even treated when the baby is still in the womb. Others can be treated soon after birth by a surgical operation or medicinal drugs. The long-term outlook for the baby could be a normal life, but certain conditions have less optimistic long-term prospects. These can affect not only the health of the baby as it grows up but also schooling and many aspects of family life.

If a couple knows they have inherited genetic disorders that can be passed on if they try for a baby, they need to discuss the risks and treatment possibilities. Their desire to have a baby may be such that they decide to go forward with the willingness to care for their child, whatever the genetic disorders. They may also consider not having children, adopting a baby, or using sperm or eggs donated from somebody without the mutation in IVF.

GENE THERAPY

A person's genes are inside every microscopic cell of their body. If there is a genetic mutation in the initial egg cell, then every cell will have the same alteration in its genes. Scientists are working on correcting these mutations with a new form of treatment called *gene therapy*.

In almost every body part, millions of tiny new cells are made every day to replace those that wear

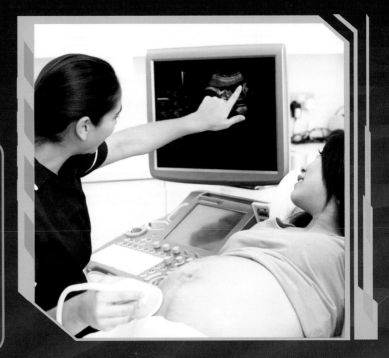

Ultrasound scans produce an image of the unborn baby that medical staff can use to check for multiple births as well as physical problems such as limb defects or missing internal organs.

out and die. With a genetic disorder, all of these cells have the same mutation. In gene therapy, the aim is to correct the mutation by replacing the affected genes with normal ones or to put in new cells that do not contain the altered genes. However, it could be dangerous to "repair" one gene without knowing what effect this might have on other genes—and ultimately on the developing baby. There may be a chance that by fixing one genetic disorder, we would create another.

STEM CELLS

One way around this difficulty is to carry out treatment before birth, when many cells of the body have not yet become specialized to do particular jobs. These unspecialized cells are called *stem cells*. These cells exist when the new life is an embryo and have the ability to grow into anything—such as skin, bone, blood, muscle. It is possible that they could be used to grow tissue for skin grafts and blood or bone marrow for transfusions. They are more likely to take up engineered genes in a permanent way and allow them to

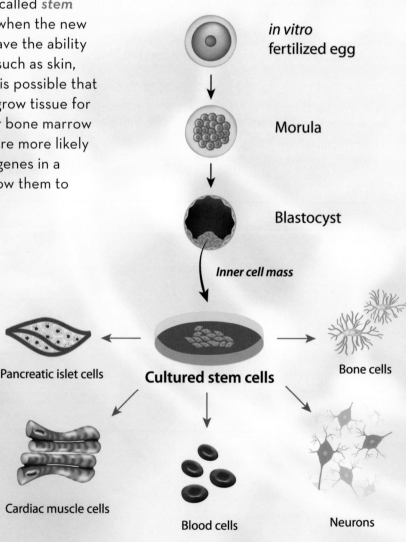

in vitro fertilized egg

Morula

Blastocyst

Inner cell mass

Pancreatic islet cells

Cultured stem cells

Bone cells

Cardiac muscle cells

Blood cells

Neurons

work. Then the genes can pass to all the cells that develop from the stem cells, sometimes for years or even a lifetime.

However, this type of treatment means testing a very tiny baby in the womb to see if it has a certain condition, which brings its own risks and problems. Progress on many genetic disorders has been slow, and some results have been disappointing thus far.

CHOOSING TRAITS

Understanding genetics can give us the chance to make choices about the children we want to have. This can go beyond the choice to have a child free from a disability or fatal condition. Some might seek to choose other, less impactful, features. Already, people can choose in some cases to have a boy or a girl. This may go as far as selecting blue eyes or more athleticism in a child. Some people feel that interfering with nature in this way is wrong, but others argue that in more extreme cases, it would be wrong not to prevent someone from having a disorder when given the chance.

DIFFICULT DECISIONS

Some serious genetic disorders can be detected while the baby is still very tiny in the womb. An example is spina bifida, where the nerves of the spinal cord and brain do not form properly. If this is detected, some parents may consider ending the pregnancy, known as *abortion*. But other parents might still have their baby and provide the additional care necessary for their child. Even if they do not have a "normal" life, they can still love and grow together as a family, as many have already done.

Views on this issue vary widely. Some countries offer abortion as part of the medical system, while others legally forbid ending a life in the womb. Some consider abortion a way of saving a child and their family from suffering. Others, especially in religious faiths, believe every person has their own unique struggles, some severe, but all have a right to life—a mother has the choice to do what she

Embryonic stem cells can grow into a baby, or be adapted for other purposes, such as to grow new skin or organs. Today, there is disagreement over whether it is acceptable to use "spare" embryos from in vitro fertilization—which could, if used differently, have turned into people—for genetic research.

wants with her body in most circumstances but not when it comes to a life-and-death decision of another human being, including if that human is the life in her body.

ABORTION DEFINED

Abortion is the ending of a pregnancy due to the death of the embryo (a developing human fewer than eight weeks old) or *fetus* (a developing human eight weeks or older) in the mother's womb. An abortion can occur naturally in what is known as a *miscarriage* or "spontaneous abortion." It can also be *induced* (caused unnaturally) by controlled medical treatment or by illegal "back-street" and homemade procedures.

QUESTIONS ABOUT ABORTION

According to the Guttmacher Institute's 2008 study, there are an estimated 43.8 million abortions performed worldwide every year. This compares to an estimated 131.4 million births per year—a ratio of one abortion for every three live births.

The World Health Organization (WHO) reported 21.6 million women experience an unsafe, often illegal, abortion in the world each year, with 86 percent of these in developing countries.

Abortion is a highly divisive topic—even in countries where abortion is

Some people believe that life should be preserved at all costs and abortion should never be allowed. Other people think that every woman has a right to choose what happens to her body—and that may include choosing to end an unhealthy, or unwanted, pregnancy.

SIDEBAR

ABORTION STATISTICS WORLDWIDE

With 2008 estimates of 22.2 million legal abortions and 21.6 million illegal, unsafe abortions each year, the approximate global monthly average is 3.65 million abortions. The proportion of abortions worldwide that take place in developing countries increased from 78 percent to 86 percent between 1995 and 2008, in part because the proportion of all women who live in developing countries increased during this period.

legal, people's opinions on the practice are divided. For example, some *pro-life* groups believe that life begins at *conception*, the very start of a pregnancy, and, therefore, abortion is a form of murder. The opposing argument from *pro-choice* campaigners is that a pregnant woman's right to choose whether or not to have an abortion should be respected. Who should have the final decision: society, doctors, or the woman herself? Should the unborn fetus's right to life be the most important factor?

TWENTIETH CENTURY SHIFT TOWARD ABORTION

Though the legal position of the United States (US) was against abortion until 1973, both rich and poor women continued to seek abortions illegally before then. Thousands died or were seriously injured due to unsanitary conditions and dangerous abortion methods.

During the 1950s and 1960s, the rise of the women's rights movement pushed the abortion debate to the forefront. Pro-choice groups lobbied governments to loosen the laws on abortion. The civil rights and antiwar movements also influenced women to fight more actively for their rights.

In 1967, two American states, Colorado and California, introduced laws to legalize abortion for a very wide range of medical reasons. In 1970, the state of New York passed the first law allowing abortion on demand up to the 24th week of pregnancy. However, illegal abortion remained common since the laws were still restrictive for women in other states.

ROE V. WADE

In 1973, Norma McCorvey—who went under the assumed name of Jane Roe—was a pregnant resident of Texas who challenged the constitutionality of the abortion laws in the state. The laws at the time made it a crime for a woman to terminate her pregnancy except on medical advice to save the life of the mother. The defendant was county District Attorney Henry Wade.

On January 22, 1973, the US Supreme Court ruled 7-2 that the Texas laws were unconstitutional under the 14th Amendment, which protected the right to privacy. The ruling declared that the right to privacy included a woman's choice to have an abortion throughout her pregnancy but balanced this against two interests of the state: protecting a woman's health and the potential for a new human life. The decision stated that until the end of the first three months of pregnancy, only a pregnant woman and her doctor have the legal right to make a decision about an abortion. After that point, it allowed state regulation of abortions. This ruling affected changes in the laws of 46 states.

REACTION OF PRO-LIFE SUPPORTERS

The *Roe vs. Wade* ruling energized the pro-life lobby. They began to demonstrate, using clinic blockades, legislative strategies, and legal challenges.

The first victory for pro-life campaigners came in July 1976, when Congress passed the Hyde Amendment. This banned Medicaid—government funding—for an abortion unless a woman's life was in danger. After this was passed, many states stopped funding abortions unless they were considered medically necessary.

Though she was instrumental in making abortion legal in the US, Norma McCorvey did not in fact have an abortion herself; she put her baby up for adoption. She has since changed her stance on the abortion debate, and in 1997, she started a pro-life outreach organization called Roe No More. In 2003, McCorvey filed a motion with the US District Court in Dallas to have the *Roe v. Wade* case overturned, presenting evidence that abortions hurt women, along with 1,000 signed statements by women saying they regretted their abortions. The court dismissed her motion the following year.

CONSENT FOR TREATMENT

In order for medical treatment to be performed, care providers need *consent*, or permission, to go forward. In the case of abortion, 2 states and Washington, DC, allow minors under age 18 to give consent; 21 states require at least one parent's consent; 13 require prior notification to at least one parent; 5 states require notification and consent from a parent; and the other states either have no relevant policy or one that is currently unenforced.

In general health care, outside of abortion, adults usually decide on the treatment they receive while parents make choices about the medical care of their children. In a hospital or clinic, adults have to sign a consent form saying that they agree to a treatment, or it cannot be carried out. Consent is not necessary in all cases. For example, if you were taken to a hospital after a serious accident, and you or your relatives were unable to give consent, emergency treatment would be carried out anyway.

Some people are unable to give informed consent—they may have an intellectual disability or simply not understand the issues,

With a lot of care and attention, many pre-term babies can be saved—but some will have serious disabilities or very poor health.

so they cannot meaningfully agree to treatment. They may also be unconscious and unable to communicate. When someone is in this position, their closest relative may be asked to give consent for necessary treatment—but there are cases in which it is not clear whether treatment is necessary.

REFUSING TREATMENT

Sometimes people do not want the treatment that can save them. Their objection may be for religious or moral reasons—they might feel that receivng organs from dead people is wrong, for example. Or, if they are very ill and in a lot of pain, they may feel that they have suffered enough and would rather die.

Occasionally, someone's decision to refuse treatment may seem wrong to everyone else. For instance, a young woman with the eating disorder anorexia nervosa may not want treatment because she genuinely believes she is too fat. Her view of her body is distorted, and though she may potentially die of starvation, she may continue to refuse food and treatment. Her relatives may seek for her to receive treatment and recover. People with mental illnesses may also feel there is nothing wrong with them and refuse treatment, though their health may suffer as a result.

IMMUNIZATIONS AND VACCINES

Modern medicine has made great advances in preventing illness and disease. Health education encourages people to take regular exercise, eat a balanced diet, limit intake of alcohol, and avoid tobacco and other drugs. Thus, we are more aware than ever of potential risks to our health. Immunization programs have gone a long way towards wiping out some of the diseases that caused many deaths in the past, such as diphtheria, measles, and tuberculosis. And large-scale programs in the developing world have eliminated smallpox and nearly wiped out polio.

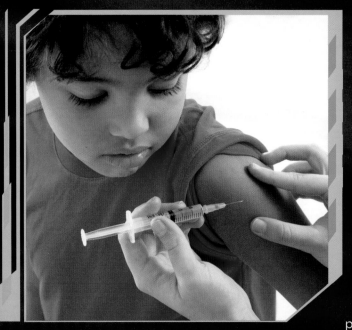

Some people are worried about possible side effects of vaccinations and would prefer not to have their children immunized against some diseases. In particular, the measles, mumps, and rubella (MMR) vaccine was refused by some parents in the past. This vaccine, used in 90 countries around the world, was linked to the developmental

According to the Centers for Disease Control and Prevention (CDC), immunization programs have saved more than a billion lives over the past 50 years.

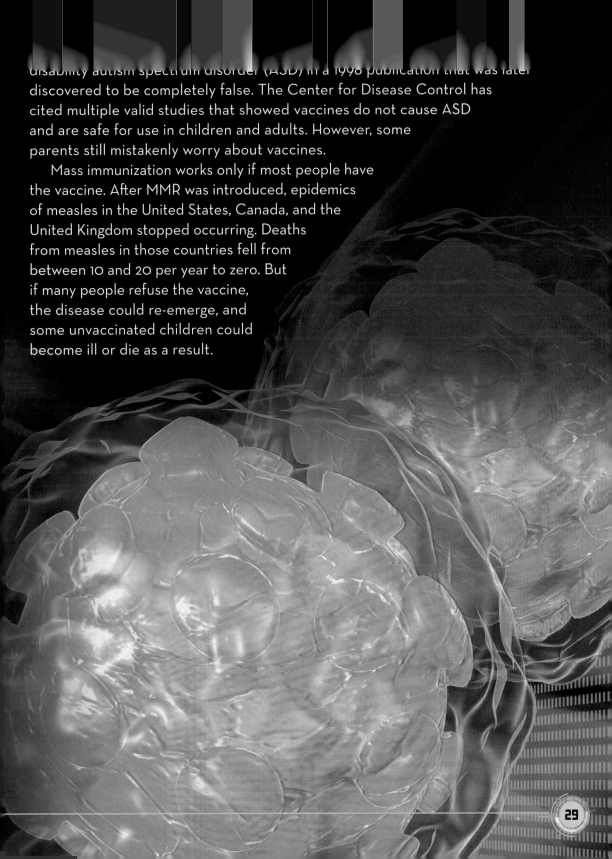

disability autism spectrum disorder (ASD) in a 1998 publication that was later discovered to be completely false. The Center for Disease Control has cited multiple valid studies that showed vaccines do not cause ASD and are safe for use in children and adults. However, some parents still mistakenly worry about vaccines.

Mass immunization works only if most people have the vaccine. After MMR was introduced, epidemics of measles in the United States, Canada, and the United Kingdom stopped occurring. Deaths from measles in those countries fell from between 10 and 20 per year to zero. But if many people refuse the vaccine, the disease could re-emerge, and some unvaccinated children could become ill or die as a result.

TEXT-DEPENDENT QUESTIONS

1. Why might stem cells have a greater success rate in gene therapy than specialized cells?

2. Name two factors that led to a 20th-century shift toward abortion in the US.

3. Describe Norma McCorvey's case, what impact it had on the US, and what her final position was years after the case.

EDUCATIONAL VIDEO

Scan here to watch a video on IVF.

Using the Internet or your school library, research the topic of when human life begins, and answer the following question: "Does human life begin at conception?"

Some believe a human life technically begins at the point of conception and should therefore be granted the right to be born without interference. From this point on, the life develops on its own, multiplying its cells and forming specific body parts, including the brain, heart, and face. It is without a doubt a living being that is human, so who can say that human life has not begun at this point? If we deny that an embryo or a fetus is a human life, we risk the danger of judging worth by ability, where babies are not as fully human as adults, or people with disabilities are not as valuable as typical people.

Others argue that a developing embryo is simply a mass of living cells. It can only be considered a full human life when it is born or at least when it is further developed. Until there is an ability to think and feel, which happens later in pregnancy, it is not yet a life. At fertilization and the early stages of growth, the mother should be able to have an abortion because the embryo or fetus is not a fully human life.

Write a two-page report, using data you have found in your research to support your conclusion, and present it to your class.

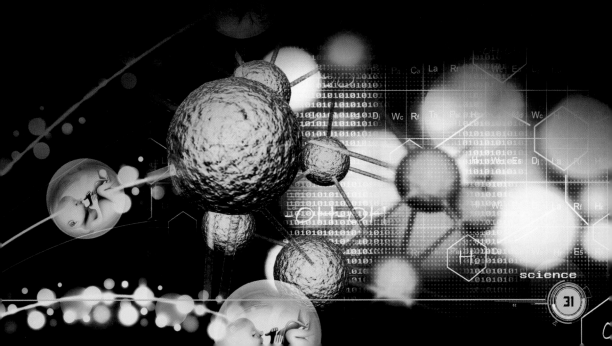

science

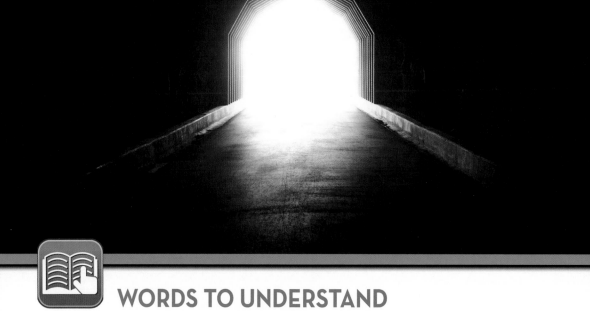

WORDS TO UNDERSTAND

assisted suicide—killing oneself with help from another person (such as a doctor) to end suffering from severe physical illness

cryonics—a procedure in which a person's body is cooled to an extremely low temperature just after he or she has died so that, in theory, the body can be restored if a cure for the cause of death is found

euthanasia—the act or practice of killing someone who is very sick or injured in order to prevent any more suffering

hospice—a place that provides a caring environment for people who are dying

living will—a document in which one says what medical decisions should be made if they become too sick or injured to make those decisions

palliative—something that reduces the effects or symptoms of a medical condition without curing it

persistent vegetative state—an unconscious state that is the result of severe brain damage and that can last for a very long time

resuscitate—to bring (someone who is unconscious, not breathing, or close to death) back to a conscious or active state again

transplant—to perform a medical operation in which an organ or other part that has been removed from the body of one person is put it into the body of another person

CHAPTER 3

QUESTIONS ABOUT THE END OF LIFE

THE MAJORITY OF CHILDREN in more developed countries, such as the United States and the United Kingdom, can look forward to 80 or more years of life. As a result, death may seem far removed as an issue of importance. Surveys in the book, *A Right to Die*, indicate that only 10 percent of 19-year-olds think about death in relation to themselves, compared to 70 percent of 65-year-olds. Yet death affects everyone sooner or later, and many young people face it directly by being a victim of an accident, terminal illness, or through a dying friend or family member.

We expect medical services to prolong life, but sometimes doctors need to choose a point at which to let someone die. Adults may refuse treatment if they are going to die and feel that treatment prolongs their suffering unnecessarily. Relatives may even make the decision to turn off a person's life-support system if doctors believe there is no chance of recovery. How can end-of-life decisions be made?

ORGAN TRANSPLANTS

Since the 1960s, surgeons have been able to carry out *transplants* on some people

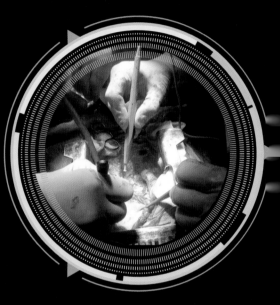

Transplants are very complex operations and a patient runs the risk of rejecting the donated organ. In many cases, donated organs such as hearts and kidneys come from car crash victims, because they are often young people with healthy organs. How would you feel about parts of your body being used after your death?

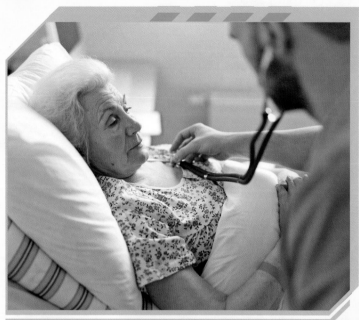

whose organs are not working properly. The process involves taking an organ such as the heart, lungs, or liver from someone who has died—or taking a non-essential organ from a living donor—and using it to replace the defective organ in a patient. Someone who receives a transplant must have treatment with medicines, so that their body does not reject the transplanted organ as a foreign part.

In most countries, patients or their relatives have to give prior permission for parts of their body to be used in transplant operations, whether they are alive or dead. Some people will not give permission—due to religious or other objections—to their organs being used after death. But many people will gladly sign up as donors knowing that they could help to save someone's life.

> *Who can judge whether it is "worth" resuscitating a very sick person whose quality of life on survival is likely to be poor?*

THE DECISION TO RESUSCITATE

If a person's heart stops beating, a specially trained medical team can often *resuscitate*, or revive, them—but they do not always do so. Family members and doctors make a case-by-case decision for each patient on whether or not to resuscitate them based on any wishes the patient had expressed in advance and the quality of life they can expect if they are resuscitated.

Resuscitation is a controversial topic not only because a person's life is at stake but also because it has serious financial consequences. Some believe hospital administrators or even family members may be pressured to not resuscitate patients because of factors such as the future cost of care, the amount of financial coverage that insurance would provide, and the number of hospital beds or clinical staff available.

FROZEN FOR THE FUTURE

Most people accept that when we die, their physical life is over forever, but some are paying large amounts of money for their dead bodies to be deep-frozen. They hope that they will be revived at some point in the future if a cure for the condition that killed them has been found. This is called *cryonics*.

Cryonics involves cooling a recently deceased person to liquid nitrogen temperatures—where physical decay essentially stops—in order to keep the body preserved indefinitely. A majority of the body's tissues remain intact at a cellular level even after the heart stops beating. With the advancement of technological and medical procedures, the hope is that future science may be able to repair or replace vital tissues and ultimately revive the patient.

NEEDS OF AGING POPULATIONS

In many developed countries, people are living longer than ever before. Advances in health care mean that people recover from, or never get, some of the diseases that would have killed them a few decades ago.

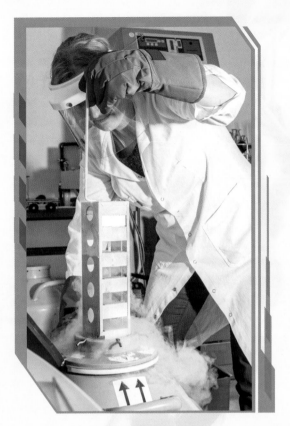

Cryonics involves cooling tissue to an extremely low temperature (below -320° Fahrenheit / -196° Celsius), in the hopes of theoretically re-animating it at some point in the future. Today there is no way to successfully revive someone who has been cryonically preserved after death. Some people believe that cryonics—an expensive yet untried process—plays on wealthy peoples' fears of death to enrich the companies that sell this technology.

But as people become elderly, they are more likely to fall ill—and if they have an accident, they are more likely to suffer a serious injury. This means that as the overall population ages, the demands for health care increase.

In some countries, the birthrate is falling while seniors are living longer and longer. This results in the average age of the population rising. Serious financial problems will occur if there are not enough young people to create the wealth needed to care for the older generation. The US faces this issue as the masses in the Baby Boomer generation are retiring, and the government will need enough money to make their social security payments.

THE EUTHANASIA QUESTION

Laws vary among countries regarding *euthanasia*—intentionally ending someone else's life to prevent further suffering. Some people are concerned that if a person could legally choose to die with assistance from others, some families may put pressure on patients to make that choice—or that soon, people would be able to more liberally choose euthanasia for others in vulnerable positions.

The word "euthanasia" comes from two words in the Greek language: *eu* means "well" or "good," and *thanatos* means "death." In modern society, euthanasia now means much more than a "good death." It has come to mean the intentional end of a person's life to end suffering.

All people die eventually, and most die of natural causes when their bodies—due to age, illness, or injury—cease to function well enough to keep them alive. Euthanasia shortens the lifespan of a person by killing them before nature runs its

 **SIDEBAR**

AN ANALOGY OF EUTHANASIA VERSUS ASSISTED SUICIDE

Dr. Jack Kevorkian, a physician famous for assisting in suicides, illustrated the difference between euthanasia and assisted suicide: "It is like giving someone a loaded gun. The patient pulls the trigger, not the doctor. If the doctor sets up the needle and syringe but lets the patient push the plunger, that's assisted suicide. If the doctor pushes the plunger, it would be euthanasia."

course. Active euthanasia occurs by an action, such as causing a person to die by giving them a lethal injection of drugs. Passive euthanasia happens through withholding food and water or not performing necessary medical care. In the US, active euthanasia is illegal in all states, but passive euthanasia is legal.

THE IMPORTANCE OF INTENTION

Euthanasia involves deliberately performing an act or deliberately not doing something with the clear intention of causing someone's death. Without intention to kill someone, euthanasia does not occur. For example, doctors are sometimes faced with a patient who is close to death. They may decide to stop a particular treatment because it no longer has any benefit to the patient's health, or they may not start a new treatment because it will not improve the patient's conditions. Some groups argue that if these decisions result in death, they are examples of passive euthanasia. However, the general opinion is that they are part of fair medical practice that is allowed by law in most countries. Since there is no intention to kill the patient, they would not be considered euthanasia.

Some people fear that society might one day use euthanasia as a way of getting rid of people no one wants to look after.

VOLUNTARY AND INVOLUNTARY EUTHANASIA

Voluntary euthanasia is when the person who is killed has made a specific request for their death. In some countries where euthanasia is legal, this request has to be made a number of times by the patient over a period of time, sometimes in written and verbal forms. In contrast, involuntary euthanasia is used to describe the killing of a person who has not clearly expressed the wish to die. Involuntary euthanasia has occurred with patients who have no ability whatsoever to communicate their wishes to caregivers, doctors, friends, or relatives. These include patients whose conditions have deteriorated to the extent that they are in a type of deep, prolonged coma that is referred to as a *persistent vegetative state (PVS)*.

THE DIFFERENCE BETWEEN EUTHANASIA AND SUICIDE

Euthanasia and suicide are not considered the same in the laws of most countries or in arguments about morals and ethics. Suicide is the intentional taking of one's own life. The final act does not involve anyone else helping in any way. With euthanasia, the assistance of another individual is required in taking a person's life.

In wealthier, more developed nations around the world, suicides are a significant cause of death. In the US, for example, the Centers for Disease Control report that, in 2013, there were 41,149 deaths due to suicide, which is 13 per 100,000 people. Suicide was the tenth leading cause of death of people in the US, with more deaths due to suicide than murder. The situation is similar in the UK, where the Office for National Statistics reported that 6,233 people took their own lives in 2013—11.9 suicides per 100,000 people.

ASSISTED SUICIDE

Assisted suicide is when a person provides the means for someone to commit suicide but leaves the final act that ends life to the person who dies. When a doctor is the person who helps, it is known as physician-assisted suicide. The person who actually performs the final action which causes death is what separates assisted suicide from euthanasia. If the person who dies performs the last act, such as the swallowing of a lethal drug prescribed by a doctor, then it is classified as assisted suicide. But if a doctor injects a person directly with a lethal drug, then it is euthanasia. While suicide is no longer illegal in most nations, assisted suicide remains a serious crime in nearly all countries of the world.

LIVING WILLS

A *living will* is a legal document that sets out how someone wishes to be treated should they become unable to communicate with their doctors. Living wills cannot legally enforce euthanasia, but they can instruct a medical team not to prolong life artificially by giving antibiotic drugs to fight an infection or connecting someone to a life-support machine. Many people argue that living wills give a patient peace of mind by making their wishes clear and taking pressure away

An advance health care directive, sometimes called a "living will," is a document in which a person explains whether or not they would like to be kept alive through artificial means in the event that their organs fail.

from doctors, friends, and family. Critics, however, wonder how it is possible or right to make a decision now for some unknown problem that may or may not occur at some point in the future.

TRENDS IN THE EUTHANASIA DEBATE

There is not one type of person who becomes a supporter for, or a critic of, euthanasia. People of all ages from all cultures and walks of life are involved in pressure and campaign groups on both sides. In the past 30 years, the number of organizations campaigning on various aspects of the issue has increased greatly.

Dozens of pro- and anti-euthanasia groups campaign by lobbying politicians, publishing books and pamphlets, using organized action, and holding rallies, meetings, and demonstrations. For example, Not Dead Yet, an anti-euthanasia group in the US, has appeared outside pro-euthanasia meetings handing out leaflets. The Patients Rights Council, an anti-euthanasia group, and Dignity in Dying, a pro-euthanasia group, are just two of many organizations that maintain large websites of information in the hope of influencing and recruiting supporters.

The words and actions of patients and family members facing the euthanasia debate can carry great weight. In the US, for instance, there was a highly publicized battle between the husband and parents of a woman with severe brain damage, Terri Schiavo, over whether she should be kept alive artificially. This prompted different right-to-life groups to join forces in order to campaign with the parents.

In contrast, one terminally ill journalist from the UK, Phil Such, attracted publicity when he went on hunger strike for a change in the law banning voluntary euthanasia. The journalist said, "I have had a great, if rather short, life. Why should this be wrecked by a long, lingering death? I am really proud of my country, yet, right at this moment, I wish to God I had been born in Holland or Oregon in the US."

SUCCESSES OF ANTI-EUTHANASIA GROUPS

Members of the anti-euthanasia lobby point to the very small number of places in the world that allow euthanasia or assisted suicide as an example of their success. Attempts to pass assisted-suicide laws in a number of American states, including New Hampshire and Maine, have failed, while the 1996 law allowing voluntary euthanasia and assisted suicide in the Northern Territory of Australia was overturned in 1998. After intense campaigning by the pressure group, Right to

Life Australia, as well as some church leaders, the federal government passed the Andrews Bill, which reversed the law in the Northern Territory. Only four people died under the law while it was in existence.

SUCCESSES OF PRO-EUTHANASIA GROUPS

Considering the fact that euthanasia was rarely discussed in the past, simply raising awareness of the issue is heralded as a major success by many euthanasia supporters. Many also believe that it is far more difficult to change the law and the way society acts than to maintain the same laws and attitudes already in place. This is why the legalization of euthanasia or assisted suicide, albeit in only a handful of places, is still viewed by many supporters as being highly significant.

The head of the Dutch Voluntary Euthanasia Society, Dr. Rob Jonquiere, said that the Dutch law of 2002 legalizing euthanasia and assisted suicide has given a major boost to similar efforts in other European countries: "Belgium has followed suit, Luxembourg has been busy and only missed legalization by one or two votes. We know they are busy in France and in the UK." Since that statement, Luxembourg legalized euthanasia and assisted suicide in its 2009 law, while France and the UK have not.

AN ALTERNATIVE WAY

In some people's view, there is an alternative to both euthanasia and keeping patients alive in intensive care units in hospitals. Known as *palliative* care, it concentrates on caring, not curing, and making terminally ill patients' last days

 **SIDEBAR**

PAINKILLING ALTERNATIVES

Dr. Eric Chevlen, Director of Palliative Care at St. Elizabeth Health Center in Ohio, stated, "We already know enough to manage virtually all cases of malignant pain successfully. The widely held belief that pain can be relieved only by doses of morphine so high as to render the patient a zombie is a myth."

SIDEBAR

THE WORLDWIDE DEBATE ON EUTHANASIA

UNITED STATES

Anti-euthanasia campaigners rally in multiple cities to protest in the US. Here, powerful pressure groups on both sides of the issue are locked in a battle to try to win the full support of the public and the government. Currently, there are no laws at the federal level on euthanasia or assisted suicide. On the state level, active euthanasia is illegal in all 50 US states, but passive euthanasia is legal. For assisted suicide—in which another person provides the means of death but does not initiate the final act that ends life—there is more allowance: 45 states consider assisted suicide illegal, and 5 states have legalized it.

FRANCE

Jacques Chirac, French President from 1995 to 2007, refused an appeal by Marie Humbert in 2002 to allow her son, Vincent, the legal right to end his life. Vincent had lost the use of his limbs as well as his sight, speech, smell, and taste in a car crash. Before his passing away in 2003, he wrote the book *I Ask the Right to Die* with the use of his right thumb, expressing his wish to die legally.

IRELAND

In 2002, mourners gathered at the funeral of Rosemary Toole Gilhooley, an Irishwoman whose death was assisted by an American minister, the Reverend George Exoo, and his assistant, Thomas McGurrin. Exoo and McGurrin traveled to Dublin, Ireland, with Toole Gilhooley, who was later found dead in the rented home they were at.

Exoo admitted that he and McGurrin helped set up a mechanism that would cut off Toole Gilhooley's oxygen supply. They also guided her through five practice sessions with it but claimed to only watch as she went through the procedure.

The two men faced extradition, or transfer from the US back to Ireland, to face charges of assisting in a suicide, but the extradition efforts failed in 2007. The death was ruled a suicide without assistance. There was swirling controversy because of Exoo and McGurrin's level of involvement in Toole Gillhooley's death.

alive as comfortable as possible. This can occur in dedicated centers for the terminally ill, known as *hospices*, which can exist in nursing homes, care centers, or at a person's own home. Pain prevention and relief is the priority, but there is also counseling and assistance for the patient, their family, and friends.

Critics point out that this care is not available to all: there are nowhere near enough beds for all terminally ill patients, and most hospices are staffed to treat just a small number of the wide range of terminal diseases that people suffer from. In response, advocates of hospices say that this is more of an issue of financing than a fault with their kind of care.

Hospice care focuses on improving the comfort and quality of life for those who are suffering from an advanced illness where recovery is unlikely.

TEXT-DEPENDENT QUESTIONS

1. Name two factors that influence whether or not medical staff resuscitates someone.

2. What is a major concern for a society that has an aging overall population?

3. Describe the differences between active euthanasia, passive euthanasia, voluntary euthanasia, and involuntary euthanasia.

4. Are euthanasia and assisted suicide the same? Why or why not?

5. Describe an alternative third way besides euthanasia or keeping someone alive in intensive care units.

EDUCATIONAL VIDEO

Scan here to watch a video on euthanasia and assisted suicide.

RESEARCH PROJECT

Using the Internet or your school library, research the topic of assisted suicide, and answer the following question: "Is there a difference between suicide and assisted suicide?"

Some claim that there is a fundamental difference. Suicide is a private act that does not involve another individual at all. Assisted suicide involves someone else helping to take a life, so another person is part of the dying process. The difference is significant and recognized by laws: suicide is not against the law in most countries, but assisted suicide is illegal in most countries.

Others contend that there is no meaningful difference between suicide and assisted suicide because the end result is the same. In both cases a person wants to end their life and eventually dies. Does it really matter that someone else was involved in the process if it is the decision of the person who dies?

Write a two-page report, using data you have found in your research to support your conclusion, and present it to your class.

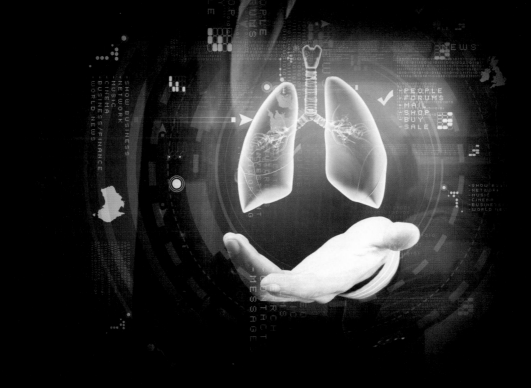

WORDS TO UNDERSTAND

clinical trial—a research study to evaluate the effectiveness and safety of medications or medical devices by monitoring their effects on one or more people

compensation—something that is done or given to make up for damage, trouble, etc.

consumerism—an attitude that values the purchase of goods that are desirable but not essential

obesity—a condition characterized by the excessive accumulation and storage of fat in the body

placebo—a pill or substance that is given to a patient like a drug but that has no physical effect on the patient

preventive medicine—a branch of medical science dealing with methods (as vaccination) of preventing the occurrence of disease

CHAPTER

THE BUSINESS OF HEALTH CARE

MEDICINE IS BIG BUSINESS. Some governments spend a lot of money on health care for their people. Others cannot afford this and do not have a centralized system to provide care. On a societal as well as individual level, the costs involved in health care lead to the burden of expenses for some and high levels of profits for others.

CONSUMERISM AND HEALTH

Consumerism—an attitude that values the purchase of goods that are desirable but not essential—can magnify health problems across an entire society. The heavy advertising of delicious but unhealthy foods—such as sweets, soft drinks, potato chips, and fast food—has caused a significant rise in diet-related health problems, of which *obesity* (having excess amount

Most people are aware when they are making unhealthy lifestyle choices. Should the government have a right to place limitations on these choices—such as increasing taxes on cigarettes or sugary drinks—for the sake of public health?

of body fat) is the forerunner. In the 1990s, for the first time in human history, the world's population of overweight people was roughly the same as the number of underfed people—about 1.1 billion. In the US in 2010, the National Institutes of Health reported more than one in three were obese, with the same rate for children. Obesity-related diseases—including cardiovascular disease, cancer, diabetes, and high blood pressure—lead to 300,000 deaths per year in the US.

DIFFERENCES BETWEEN COUNTRIES

In the United Kingdom, people who earn more than a minimum wage pay for the National Health Service (NHS) through taxes. The NHS aims to give everyone all the treatment they need for free. Because of the demands on this type of health care, some people also buy private health insurance. This means that they pay an insurance company to cover the costs if they want to be treated more quickly or to stay in a more comfortable hospital than they can get through the NHS.

In the United States, there is no free health insurance provided by the federal government like the NHS. Most people buy

The Affordable Care Act of 2010 was intended to provide greater access to health insurance for all Americans. However, many people have protested against the legislation, claiming that it has led to greater costs for businesses and the middle class.

private insurance that will help pay for any treatments they need. Free hospitals are available for people who cannot afford insurance, but they may be less comfortable and not as well equipped.

In 2010, President Barack Obama signed into law the Patient Protection and Affordable Care Act (PPACA), which is sometimes called "Obamacare." Its goal is to give US citizens access to affordable, quality health insurance and to reduce the growth in health care spending.

The ACA expands the affordability, quality, and availability of private and public health insurance through consumer protections and other benefits: young adults can stay on their parents' plans until age 26; insurance companies cannot deny coverage or drop a person based on health status; the federal government offers each state extra funding to expand Medicaid, which insures people under the poverty level; tax breaks are offered to small businesses that provide health insurance to their employees; and health

In 2014, a social media phenomenon known as the "ice bucket challenge" raised more than $200 million for research into a disease called amyotrophic lateral sclerosis (ALS). Scientists have credited this unexpected funding with accelerating their research on ALS, leading to breakthroughs in their understanding of the disease.

insurance marketplaces were created to streamline the application process, where people can compare competitively priced health plans and receive tax benefits for signing up.

In some countries, private health care systems are widely used. However, in many developing countries, there is no free system and no health care offered to the poorest people. Even in private hospitals where patients pay money out of pocket, the treatments available often do not match those in developed countries.

FUNDING RESEARCH

New medical treatments are expensive to develop. If companies think they will make a profit from their research, they will invest more money in it. This usually means looking for cures for diseases that kill many people, such as cancer. Medicines for common ailments such as headaches and colds can also generate much money. Most of us willingly buy these treatments—just to make our lives more comfortable—so it is worthwhile for drug companies to develop them.

There are health care areas in which research is severely lacking simply because less money would be made from any treatments developed. Rare illnesses, for example, affect too few people for medical companies to benefit. Illnesses that mostly affect people in poor countries make small profits because those afflicted cannot afford expensive treatments. Even areas such as mental health are neglected because they are less in the public eye. Much research for these treatments has to be funded by charities because governments and medical companies will not pay.

THE COST OF HEALTH CARE

Health care is expensive. As we have seen, in some countries people have to pay for their own treatment or apply for insurance to cover the costs. In other countries, health care is free to anyone who needs it, paid for by the government which collects money through taxes. In some developing countries, there is no money for health care at all.

Preventive medicine—working to avoid disease in the first place—does not make drug companies much money, but it is a useful investment for

governments, as fewer people would need expensive treatments later on. The problem is the difficulty of getting people to change their lifestyles to avoid possible dangers they may not understand. In this field, health care and education must work close together for successful results.

Companies that develop new drugs and treatments are usually motivated in large part to make money. Many of the treatments they produce cost so much that some countries just cannot afford them. People in the developing world often die from diseases that could easily be cured given the funding. Even in a wealthy place like the UK, the NHS cannot pay for some of the treatments that would help many people. This means some patients go without the best treatment and may even die.

PUBLIC AND PRIVATE HEALTH CARE

There are advantages and disadvantages to both public health care—paid for by the government with taxes—and private health care systems—paid for by individuals. Some people say that where health care is free, people demand more of it than they would if they had to pay. They may seek help for minor problems that they might otherwise ignore and expect quick, high-quality treatment, forgetting how many others are demanding the same thing. In reality, people often have to wait a long time for free treatment if their condition is not life-threatening.

Where private systems are in operation, treatments may be given sooner. But as people get older, or if they develop a medical condition that cannot be completely cured, the cost of their health insurance increases—sometimes to the point where they cannot afford it any more. If someone cannot afford insurance or payments for the treatments they need, they will face financial difficulties if they fall ill.

Most people accept that there is a limit to the amount of money any country can spend on health care. This means that there will always be choices to be made. In a country such as the UK, where everyone contributes to the cost of health care, everyone has an interest in how the available money is spent. Some people object to spending it on treatments they do not consider especially important—fertility programs, for example. Others question whether we should buy very expensive medicines and treatments to prolong the life of people with illnesses that cannot ultimately be cured.

PAYING FOR HEALTH CARE

Some health problems can be traced to particular aspects of modern living. If someone suffers an accident at work, they can often claim *compensation* from their employer for their injury. Perhaps the employer should also pay for their treatment. Some problems can be traced to certain industries too. The tobacco industry causes serious health conditions and costs countries a great deal in medical care for smokers. Many people think that fumes from traffic exhaust have caused an increase in childhood asthma.

Adding a tax to some products to pay for the health care needs they create is a possible solution to covering expenses, but it would raise the prices of these items. This might mean, for instance, paying more for gasoline to help fund asthma treatment or an extra tax on tobacco to cover treatment of smoking-related illnesses. Governments are careful to set taxation at an appropriate level to get as much money from the tax as they can while not overburdening taxpayers. If the tax on, say, alcohol, was too high, people may buy less of it, resulting in the government collecting less tax money overall.

SIDEBAR

ANIMALS AND ROBOTICS

Animals may be used in the development of medical technology as well as for testing treatments. Scientists have implanted electrodes into the brains of monkeys to intercept electrical signals sent by the brain when the monkey moves its limbs. By working with these signals, they have been able to get a robotic arm to move in the same way as the monkey's own arm. Researchers hope to use this technology to enable people to move artificial limbs by simply thinking—just as they would move a real limb.

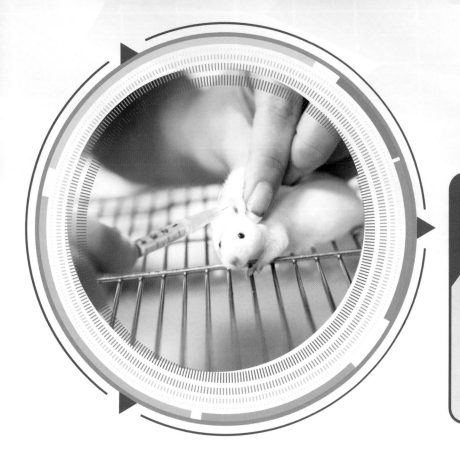

TESTING, TESTING

Before a new treatment can be used, it has to be tested to make sure it is safe. Even then, mistakes are sometimes made, with potential harm to masses of people.

In the late 1950s and early 1960s, many pregnant women were given a drug called Thalidomide to cure morning sickness (being sick during pregnancy). But Thalidomide interfered with the development of the baby, and some of the women gave birth to children with serious limb deformities. It took some time for people to realize and accept that Thalidomide was responsible, as doctors had not been careful to track what treatments they had given to women.

There have been many other cases since of medicines having unwanted side effects—but few have been as serious as Thalidomide. Now, all medicines in the US must be tested thoroughly before they can be accepted for general use.

There are several stages in the testing of modern medicines. First, they may be tested on simple living cells in a laboratory to make sure they do what they are supposed to do. Then, they may be tested on animals, not only in normal doses, but also in very large doses given over a long period of time. Finally, clinical trials are carried out on human patients.

ANIMAL TESTING

Specially bred animals—often mice, dogs, and monkeys—are used at different stages of the testing process for new medicines and other treatments. Medical researchers involved in animal testing claim that it is often the only way they can test new treatments thoroughly. If they had tested Thalidomide on pregnant mice, for example, perhaps the problems with human children would have been detected earlier. They say that they are justified in using animals if the results of their work will save human lives or relieve human suffering.

People who are against animal testing say that much of the work could be carried out on tissue cultures—samples of body tissue grown in a lab—instead of making animals suffer. Many say that we do not have the right to make animals suffer, and some religions forbid killing animals or causing them pain or stress. Already, testing of cosmetics on animals has been greatly reduced because of public opinion. If enough people objected to testing medical treatments on animals, maybe this too would stop in time.

CLINICAL TRIALS

To begin a *clinical trial* to test a new treatment, a committee of experts must examine and approve the proposal. Then, those who will be tested have to sign for consent to be a subject in the test.

When starting a clinical trial, one group of patients is given a new treatment and a similar group is given an identical-looking *placebo*—a "medicine" that has no effect. In this way, no one can tell whether or not they are getting the real medicine. The doctors or nurses who give people the treatment—or placebo—do not know which is which either, so their own knowledge cannot affect the results of the test.

After a period of treatment, all the patients are tested in the same ways. From the results, the researchers can find out if the medicine actually produces the intended healing effect and if it has any unwanted side effects.

The process of testing medicines takes a very long time, often many years. While a drug is being tested, it cannot be legally prescribed, as it has not been approved as safe and effective for general use. Yet someone who has a terminal illness may be willing to try an experimental treatment, even if it has not been proven to work and could produce horrible side effects. Approval of tested drugs could come too late for certain patients, so some agree to use the treatment and release the medical staff and drug companies from responsibility, should anything go wrong.

New drugs undergo rigorous testing in laboratories before they are approved for use in humans. At first, the drugs are only dispensed in carefully monitored clinical trials, often involving volunteer patients, so that any side effects or unexpected consequences can be observed.

Hospitals and researchers are closely watched to make sure that people are treated fairly and ethically during clinical trials. In the past, this has not always been the case. During the 1950s, for example, the US Army tested soldiers with large doses of radiation in order to find out if it had any harmful effects. Many of the soldiers later fell ill or died as a result. The knowledge we have gained from this has been valuable, but the cost of soldiers' lives is something that cannot be paid with money. Now, many tests are conducted and must prove to be safe before human subjects are used in trials.

TEXT-DEPENDENT QUESTIONS

1. Identify four health care benefits to citizens provided by Obamacare.
2. What is an experimental treatment, and why might some patients elect to use it?

 EDUCATIONAL VIDEO

Scan here to watch a video on how health insurance works.

RESEARCH PROJECT

Using the Internet or your school library, research the topic of public and private health care, and answer the following question: "Should the US adopt a public health care system?"

Some contend that the US has always had a private health care system and should keep it that way. Each individual should pay for health insurance according to what they can afford and get the benefits they pay for. This way, people receive what they earn in a fair system.

Others argue that the US should adopt a public health care system because health care is a right that should be afforded to all people, not a privilege that only the wealthy can have. Education is a right that the government provides for the public, but basic health is even more of a fundamental need. Many countries around the world have a public health care system that works, and they have prevented insurance companies from profiting off of sick people and controlling who gets care and who is denied.

Write a two-page report, using data you have found in your research to support your conclusion, and present it to your class.

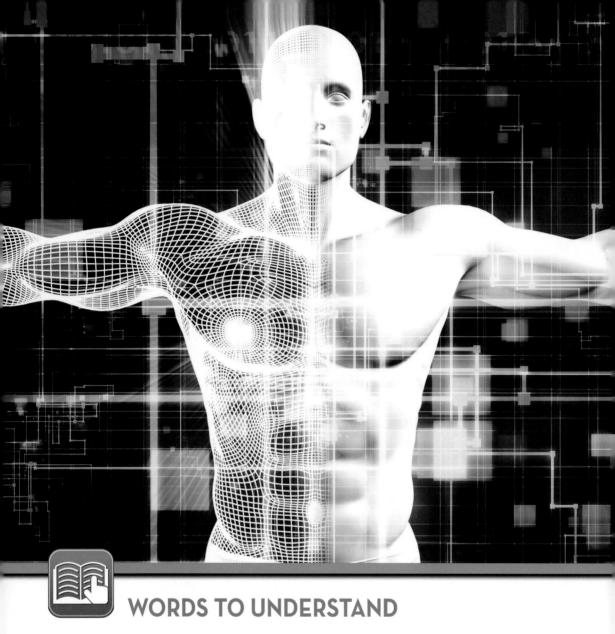

WORDS TO UNDERSTAND

clone—a plant or animal that is grown from one cell of its parent and that has exactly the same genes as its parent

vested interest—a personal or private reason for wanting something to be done or to happen

xenotransplant—the transplantation of an organ, tissue, or cells between two different species, especially from an animal to a human

CHAPTER 5

MOVING TOWARD THE FUTURE

SCIENTISTS ARE FINDING MORE AND MORE resources for new medical treatments. If you became very ill, you may care more about whether a treatment will cure you than where it came from or how it was developed. But as a society, we set limits based on what we believe is ethical. How do we balance what we consider right or fair with our desire to cure as many people as possible?

STEM CELL RESEARCH

Stem cells are the first cells produced when a fertilized human egg begins to divide. They are the cells that would develop into a whole human baby if the embryo were left to grow in the mother's body. At the earliest stage, all the cells are exactly the same, but each has the information and potential to grow into any kind of cell in the human body. As the embryo grows, the stem cells specialize and become cells for internal organs, skin, blood, bone, and every other body part.

The growth potential of stem cells makes them extremely valuable for medical research. Because they are not yet specialized, they can be "programmed" to become any type of cell. Some scientists believe that we should be able to work from stem cells to create, for example, real skin to use in skin grafts and treatments for conditions such as diabetes.

CLONING

Our bodies are designed to reject foreign tissue. This means that people who receive organ transplants have to be given medicines to prevent their bodies from rejecting the new material. Through *cloning*—creating living things that have exactly the same genes—we may be able to avoid this problem. Cloning can be done by using embryonic stem cells to make duplicate cells or taking specialized adult cells and "switching on or off" certain genes to create the desired type of

SIDEBAR

HELLO, DOLLY!

Dolly the sheep was born in July, 1996, in Edinburgh, Scotland. She was not the first clone of an animal, but she was the first mammal to be cloned from a specialized cell taken from an adult. Dolly showed that, in principle, any cell from any animal or plant, even an adult, could be used to make a clone. She died in 2003, due to problems usually found in much older sheep. Premature aging is common in cloned animals.

cells. A clone has exactly the same genetic makeup as its "parent," so anything cloned would be accepted by the parent's body.

The technology exists to make human clones and genetically engineer human cells. Cloned human embryos have in fact already been produced. Should this work continue, or are the potential consequences too dangerous? Would human clones grow up to look and behave exactly the same as each other? What if a top soldier is cloned to produce a world-dominating army?

At the moment, stem cells can only be used from embryos left over from IVF programs. Some people believe that a fertilized egg counts as a human baby. Whether or not a fertilized egg should be considered a human life depends on when you think life begins. The Catholic Church teaches that life begins as soon as the egg is fertilized. Traditional Jewish belief is that life begins when the baby's head has emerged at birth. Other people place the start of life at different points in between these stages, many around 90 days after fertilization.

TRANSPLANT POSSIBILITIES

In 2016, there were 121,000 people in the US on the waiting list for a life-saving organ transplant. Every 10 minutes, someone is added to the national transplant waiting list, and 22 people die each day while waiting for a transplant. As there are not enough organs, scientists have tried to find new ways of getting the body parts needed.

One area now being researched is the use of animal organs. Scientists have learned that pigs' bodies are very similar to humans'. Medical researchers have discovered that organs transplanted into humans from pigs are less likely to be rejected than those from other animals. Specially treated pigskin makes a superb temporary bandage on human burns because it prevents infection and allows the patient's damaged skin to repair itself. Scientists have not yet worked out a way of getting hold of a pig's heart, kidney, or skin that does not negatively affect the pig. Eventually, we may be able to use organs from pigs to transplant into people.

Genetic engineering involves changing the genes of a plant or animal to alter some of its characteristics. Scientists have created genetically engineered pigs whose hearts will not be rejected by the human body. Perhaps animal organs, such as livers or kidneys, could be injected with human genes, so that the body of a person receiving one of them in a transplant would not reject it. *Xenotransplants*, animal-to-human transplants, could one day be a way of treating patients who now have to wait until a suitable human organ becomes available.

MEDICAL FARMS

It is not just transplant organs that can be "grown" through other animals. We already use different species to create some medicines.

One of the early successes of genetic engineering in medicine was the production of the hormone insulin. People with diabetes lack insulin, which controls the way the body uses its main energy source, sugar. As a result, they can become very ill or even die from diabetes. To keep them healthy, they need frequent injections of insulin to process sugar in their bodies.

The normal treatment is to replace the missing insulin with regular injections. Insulin for these injections used to be obtained from farm animals such as pigs. However, those forms of insulin are slightly different from the human type. In the 1980s, the gene for making human insulin was identified and put into *E. coli* bacteria. These bacteria were able to use the gene as their "instructions" for making human insulin for injection.

Genetic engineering has also been used to produce clotting factor, which can be given to people with the genetic condition hemophilia—where a person's blood does not clot and keeps bleeding—so that their blood clots normally. By using this clotting factor, hemophiliacs avoid the need for blood transfusions, which carry the risk of infections from contaminated blood, such as AIDS and hepatitis. Microbes have been genetically engineered to make antibiotic drugs that kill germs and stop infectious diseases. They can also produce the drug interferon, which treats some diseases caused by viruses and fights certain types of cancer. Some of the vaccines given to babies and children for lifelong protection against diseases are also products of genetic engineering.

SIDEBAR

MEDICAL FARMING INNOVATIONS

Genetic engineers are currently working on new ideas that could improve health for the masses:

- Protein-enriched potatoes in India that may nourish underfed children who do not get enough protein in their usual diet
- Cows whose is milk very similar to human breast milk, so women who cannot breastfeed their babies have an alternative
- Mosquitoes that are resistant to malaria or become infertile if infected with malaria, preventing its spread to humans

PUBLIC HEALTH VS. PRIVATE CHOICES

We are not all the same and we do not all want the same things. Yet some of our health care choices are made by governments or other bodies who act for everyone at once. Most countries have departments of public health. These are government departments with the responsibility of keeping the public as healthy as possible through actions that affect everyone. How do we balance individual choices with public health actions that may benefit an entire society?

Most of us feel that our health is a personal matter. We generally want details of our bodies to be private, and as individuals, we want choices regarding the way our health care is handled. But governments have to plan public health care for the future, and to do this they need details about us. They also want to streamline the treatments to make the medical system as efficient, quick, and cheap as possible. Sometimes a compromise is needed, but it is not always something we are happy with.

If you go to a doctor for help with a common problem, he or she may offer you a fairly standard treatment proven to be effective on many other people. Unless you have special medical knowledge, you are not likely to know of any other options. Sometimes, there are alternative treatments that may cost more and so are not offered to people. You might want to try a different type of treatment such as acupuncture. But you may not be told about it because your doctor may be suspicious of techniques that have not been tested as thoroughly as "standard"

medicines. Even if you were told, you may have to pay privately for this different kind of treatment.

ONLINE MEDICINE

More and more people have been accessing the Internet to find

Issues that seem totally unrelated to medicine can still affect our health. By causing pollution, traffic becomes a health problem as well as a transport issue.

information on medical problems and remedies. Some even try to work out medical solutions for themselves if they do not feel well.

The Internet can be a valuable source of self-help and a useful way to communicate with other sufferers. People with a rare condition who may not have someone to talk to locally may be able to find another with the same condition online.

Some doctors find it threatening or difficult to deal with patients who have researched their illnesses on websites. The doctors may not be able to offer some of the treatments the patients have read about, or the patient may have used an unreliable source—or misunderstood the information they found—and wrongly identified their illness. Patients may also try to treat themselves without the advice of a medical professional, lacking awareness of complications or treatment side effects. As we move deeper into a digital society, these types of issues may become a bigger problem.

> *Does medical information on the Internet empower patients or make doctors' lives more difficult?*

LEGAL PROTECTION

Regulations about who may practice medicine are intended to protect us from being served by people who are underqualified or even intend harm. These rules change over time to keep up with the needs of society. In the US, for example, the demands on doctors in hospitals is increasing, so changes have been made to allow some nursing staff to carry out procedures that previously only doctors were allowed to do. By law, the nurses are now trained and tested to meet required standards for these procedures.

National laws to protect health do not just affect medical services. They apply to many other aspects of life too—how long we are allowed to work without a break for food or rest, which pesticides farmers may use, how food should be packaged and stored in shops, and so on.

Although most laws are specific to individual countries, there is global agreement about some matters. The World Health Organization (WHO) and World Medical Association (WMA) are two international bodies that work to increase health around the world. The WHO works in the areas of medicine, famine, and poverty with the aim to eradicate disease and offer all people "a state of complete physical, mental, and social well-being." The WMA has declared that all doctors must make the following promises: "I will practice my profession with conscience and dignity; the health of my patient will be my first consideration; I will respect the secrets which are confided in me, even after the patient has died…. I will not permit consideration of religion, nationality, race, party, politics, or social standing to intervene between my duty and my patient; I will maintain the utmost respect for human life from its beginning, even under threat, and I will not use my medical knowledge contrary to the laws of humanity…."

Human Stem Cell Applications

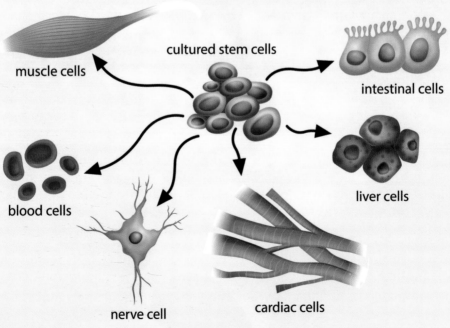

muscle cells

cultured stem cells

intestinal cells

blood cells

liver cells

nerve cell

cardiac cells

LAWS AND LIFESTYLE

Our lifestyles affect our health in many ways. Most governments use laws to protect the health of the people in their countries. For example, a law that says you must wear a seatbelt in a car is intended to reduce the number of deaths and injuries in road accidents. We have laws that forbid the use of many drugs because they are harmful to our health. There are regulations that say food in restaurants must be prepared in hygienic conditions to protect us from food poisoning.

The government cannot protect our health entirely. We also have to make intelligent choices and act wisely. Some people think that the government interferes too much with our lives, and we should be given more choice in how we live. Others think it is beneficial to have many laws to protect us and our health—especially in countries where everyone shares the cost of the public's medical treatment.

ETHICS COMMITTEES

We have seen throughout this book how our health is governed by many different aspects of our lives—our living conditions, food, the environment, and so on. But who is monitoring the care we receive from health services or the risks posed to us by different industries that affect our well-being? How much responsibility do we have for the health of other people around the world?

Ethics committees are groups of people who meet to discuss the work carried out by scientists in research institutions and hospitals. An ethics committee tries to represent the views of everyone who will have an interest in an issue and make decisions about what is right and wrong—or what is allowed and what is not. They discuss individual cases as well as more abstract issues. An ethics committee in a hospital might review the case of an individual patient, or it might be appointed by the government to investigate whether or not research into a particular area should be permitted. Each country may draw up its own laws, and in some areas of research, these can differ considerably. At the moment, certain medical procedures are legal in some places but not in others.

Many of the people working in controversial fields like genetics have a **vested** *interest*—they may be trying to make money or further their own careers. But in a specialized area, these people, who may be biased, are the ones who often know most about the issues. How they explain things can make a huge difference to society because our opinions depend on the information they supply. We need to be sure we are basing our views on balanced facts and not on biased arguments. The more informed we are about health care issues, the more capable we will be in creating balanced guidelines for future medical treatments.

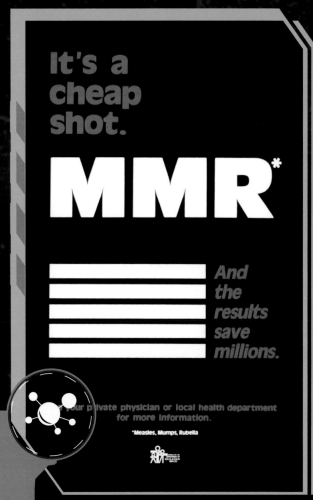

It's a cheap shot.

MMR*

And the results save millions.

...your private physician or local health department for more information.

*Measles, Mumps, Rubella

Governments often use posters, such as this one promoting vaccination from the state of Washington, as part of publicity campaigns intended to encourage citizens to be healthy.

TEXT-DEPENDENT QUESTIONS

1. Name two key medical products developed from genetic engineering.

2. What are two problems that can arise from people researching their own medical conditions online?

 EDUCATIONAL VIDEO

Scan here to watch a video on the science behind cloning.

RESEARCH PROJECT

Using the Internet or your school library, research the topic of reproductive human cloning, and answer the following question: "Should human cloning be allowed to create cloned, living people?"

Some believe that if we have the technology to clone humans, we should be able to do it. If a couple is infertile, they can have a child that is biologically connected to them. Parents whose child dies could have that child "back" through cloning. Though human cloning is not developed or safe now, if it becomes safe, it is a right that people have to do what is within their means.

Others maintain that cloning humans should not be allowed because it would take away from the diversity of human life, which is a benefit to society. Cloning would lead to a culture where humans are treated as objects that can be manufactured and designed rather than created. It is also unsafe: most cloning attempts in animals lead to miscarriages, stillbirths, and risks to the carrying mother, and no humans should be put at risk in such ways.

Write a two-page report, using data you have found in your research to support your conclusion, and present it to your class.

SERIES GLOSSARY OF KEY TERMS

anomaly—something that differs from the expectations generated by an established scientific idea. Anomalous observations may inspire scientists to reconsider, modify, or come up with alternatives to an accepted theory or hypothesis.

evidence—test results and/or observations that may either help support or help refute a scientific idea. In general, raw data are considered evidence only once they have been interpreted in a way that reflects on the accuracy of a scientific idea.

experiment—a scientific test that involves manipulating some factor or factors in a system in order to see how those changes affect the outcome or behavior of the system.

hypothesis—a proposed explanation for a fairly narrow set of phenomena, usually based on prior experience, scientific background knowledge, preliminary observations, and logic.

natural world—all the components of the physical universe, as well as the natural forces at work on those things.

objective—to consider and represent facts without being influenced by biases, opinions, or emotions. Scientists strive to be objective, not subjective, in their reasoning about scientific issues.

observe—to note, record, or attend to a result, occurrence, or phenomenon.

science—knowledge of the natural world, as well as the process through which that knowledge is built through testing ideas with evidence gathered from the natural world.

subjective—referring to something that is influenced by biases, opinions, and/

or emotions. Scientists strive to be objective, not subjective, in their reasoning about scientific issues.

test—an observation or experiment that could provide evidence regarding the accuracy of a scientific idea. Testing involves figuring out what one would expect to observe if an idea were correct and comparing that expectation to what one actually observes.

theory—a broad, natural explanation for a wide range of phenomena in science. Theories are concise, coherent, systematic, predictive, and broadly applicable, often integrating and generalizing many hypotheses. Theories accepted by the scientific community are generally strongly supported by many different lines of evidence. However, theories may be modified or overturned as new evidence is discovered.

FURTHER READING

ABORTION

Erdreich, Sarah. *Generation Roe: Inside the Future of the Pro-Choice Movement.* New York: Seven Stories Press, 2013.

Fisher, Brian E. *Abortion: The Ultimate Exploitation of Women.* New York: Morgan James Publishing, 2013.

Grady, John. *Abortion: Yes or No?* Charlotte, NC: TAN Books, 2015.

Johnson, Abby. *The Walls Are Talking: Former Abortion Clinic Workers Tell Their Stories.* San Francisco: Ignatius Press, 2016.

Pollitt, Katha. *Pro: Reclaiming Abortion Rights.* New York: Picador, 2014.

EUTHANASIA

Beville, Kieran. *Dying to Kill: A Christian Perspective on Euthanasia and Assisted Suicide.* Cambridge, OH: Christian Publishing House, 2014.

Butler, Katy. *Knocking on Heaven's Door: The Path to a Better Way of Death.* New York: Scribner, 2014.

Chell, Byron. *Aid in Dying The Ultimate Argument: The Clear Ethical Case for Physician Assisted Death.* North Charleston, SC: CreateSpace, 2014.

Haerens, Margaret. *Euthanasia (Opposing Viewpoints).* Farmington Hills, MI: Greenhaven Press, 2015.

Prokofieff, Sergei O., and Peter Seleg. *Honoring Life: Medical Ethics and Physician-Assisted Suicide.* Herndon, VA: SteinerBooks, 2014.

GENETIC ENGINEERING

Carey, Nessa. *The Epigenetics Revolution: How Modern Biology Is Rewriting Our Understanding of Genetics, Disease, and Inheritance.* New York: Columbia University Press, 2013.

Knoepfler, Paul. *Stem Cells: An Insider's Guide.* Singapore: World Scientific Publishing Company, 2013.

Slack, Jonathan. *Stem Cells: A Very Short Introduction.* Oxford: Oxford University Press, 2012.

HEALTHY LIFESTYLES

Lusk, Jayson. *Unnaturally Delicious: How Science and Technology Are Serving Up Super Foods to Save the World.* New York: St. Martin's Press, 2016.

Lustig, Robert H. *Fat Chance: Beating the Odds against Sugar, Processed Food, Obesity, and Disease.* New York: Hudson Street Press, 2012.

INTERNET RESOURCES

ABORTION

Pro-Life Websites

http://www.nrlc.org/ National Right to Life deals with many pro-life causes but concentrates on abortion matters.

http://www.feministsforlife.org/ Feminists for Life of America is pro-woman and pro-life, dedicated to systematically eliminating the root causes that drive women to abortion—primarily lack of practical resources and support—through holistic, woman-centered solutions.

http://lifecharity.org.uk/ Life is the largest pro-life organization in the UK, combining advocacy and education with a nationwide care service. They support anyone facing a crisis pregnancy, pregnancy loss, or after-effects of an abortion.

http://prolifeaction.org/ The Pro-Life Action League aims to save unborn children through non-violent direct action, including public protests, promoting activism, and youth outreach.

Pro-Choice Websites

https://www.plannedparenthood.org/ Planned Parenthood has information on abortion—how to decide whether abortion is right for you, descriptions of the procedures and risks, and supporting information for friends, parents, or partners of a woman seeking abortion.

http://www.reproductiverights.org/ The Center for Reproductive Rights uses the law to advance reproductive freedom as a fundamental human right that all governments are legally obligated to protect, respect, and fulfill.

https://www.guttmacher.org/ The Guttmacher Institute is a leading research and policy organization committed to advancing sexual and reproductive health and rights in the US and globally.

http://www.fwhc.org The Feminist Women's Health Center maintains an extensive website with information about abortion procedures, personal stories, and poetry.

EUTHANASIA

http://euthanasia.procon.org/ A comprehensive website that provides pros and cons to euthanasia and physician-assisted suicide, including definitions, practical concerns, religious points of view, legal considerations, and historical information.

http://www.religioustolerance.org/euth_wld.htm A balanced website with information on the history of euthanasia, the situation in a number of countries, and the arguments for and against.

http://www.patientsrightscouncil.org/site/ Formerly called the International Task Force on Euthanasia and Assisted Suicide, the Patients Rights Council is a US-based organization opposing euthanasia. The website contains many fact sheets and details of specific cases and campaigns.

http://www.dignityindying.org.uk/
Campaign for assisted suicide with news, opinions, legal information, resources, and personal stories.

http://www.euthanasia.com Large and comprehensive website offering articles, debate topics, and cases that are presented from an anti-euthanasia perspective.

http://www.dignitas.ch/
Dignitas promotes euthanasia and has news and videos from around the world for its campaign.

http://www.epcc.ca/ The Euthanasia Prevention Coalition has newsletters, petitions, book recommendations, resources, and blogs that oppose euthanasia.

GENETIC ENGINEERING

http://www.gmo-compass.org/eng/home/ GMO Compass provides a wide variety of GMO information on topics such as grocery shopping, human health, and environmental safety.

http://www.geneticsandsociety.org/index.php Center for Genetics and Society's website on stem cell research, cloning, and genetic engineering on animals. Includes policies on genetics at the federal and state levels in the US, as well as regulations in other countries.

https://www.genome.gov/10001772 National Human Genome Research Institute's information on the human genome, including a timeline, overview of the Human Genome Project, and implications for the future.

INDEX

abortion, 16, 23-27
    number performed annually, 24, 25
    research project about, 31
advance health care directive, **39**
    See also living wills
Affordable Care Act, **48**, 49-50
American Medical Association (AMA), 38
Andrews Bill (Australia), 41
animals
    and medical research, 53, **54**, 55
    and transplants, 62-63
assisted suicide, 32, 36, 39, 40-41, 42
    research project about, 45
    See also euthanasia

Centers for Disease Control and Prevention (CDC), **28**, 29, 38
Chevlen, Eric, 41
Chirac, Jacques, 42
clinical trials, 46, 55-57
    See also research, medical
clones, 60, 61-62, 71
consent, informed, 26-27
consumerism, 46, 47-48
cryonics, 32, 35
cystic fibrosis (CF), 20

Dignity in Dying (organization), 40
disorders, genetic, 19-20, 21-22, 23
Dolly the sheep, 62
Dutch Voluntary Euthanasia Society, 41

embryos, 16, 17, 19, 24, 31
    and stem cells, 22-23, 61, 62
ethics, 6, 7, 9, 23, 68-69
    and fertility treatments, 18-19
euthanasia, 32, 36-38, 39
    opposition to, 38, 40-41, 42
    See also assisted suicide
Exoo, George, 42

fertility treatments, 17-19
    in vitro fertilization, 16, 18-19, **23**, 62
fetuses, 16, 24, 31
    See also embryos

France, 42

gene therapy, 20, 21-22
    definition of, 16
genes, 61-62
    definition of, 16
    and disorders, 19-20, 21-22, 23
    and mutation, 16, 20, 21-22
genetic disorders, 19-20, 23
    treatment of, 21-22
    See also genes
genetic engineering, 63-64
Gilhooley, Rosemary Toole. *See* Toole Gilhooley, Rosemary
government
    and the environment, 9-10
    and health care, 9-10, 47, 48-49, 50-51, 65, 68

health care
    and aging populations, 35-36
    and consent, 26-27
    costs of, 47-52
    decisions regarding, 10, 12-13, 34-35, 52, 65
    and ethics, 6, 7, 9, 18-19, 23, 68-69
    and fertility treatments, 16, 17-19, **23**, 62
    global, 12-13, 51, 67
    and government, 9-10, 47, 48-49, 50-51, 65, 68
    and the Internet, 65-66
    and legal issues, 66-68
    and organ transplants, **8**, 32, 33-34, 60, 62-63
    and palliative care, 32, 41, 43
    and preventive medicine, 46, 50-51
    "public" vs. "private," 51-52, 59
    and refusing treatment, 27-28
    See also research, medical; treatments, medical
hospice, 32, 43
Humbert, Marie, 42
Hyde Amendment, 26

I Ask the Right to Die (Humbert), 42
"ice bucket challenge," **49**
immunizations. *See* vaccinations
in vitro fertilization, 16, 18-19, **23**, 62
informed consent, 26-27

ABOUT THE AUTHOR

Beatrice Kavanaugh is a graduate of Bryn Mawr College. A former newspaper writer and editor, she currently works as a freelance writer. This is her first book.

PUBLISHER'S NOTE

The websites that are cited in this book were active at the time of publication. The publisher is not responsible for websites that have changed their address or discontinued operation since the date of publication. The publisher reviews and updates websites each time the book is reprinted.

PHOTO CREDITS